D0118877

# Insects

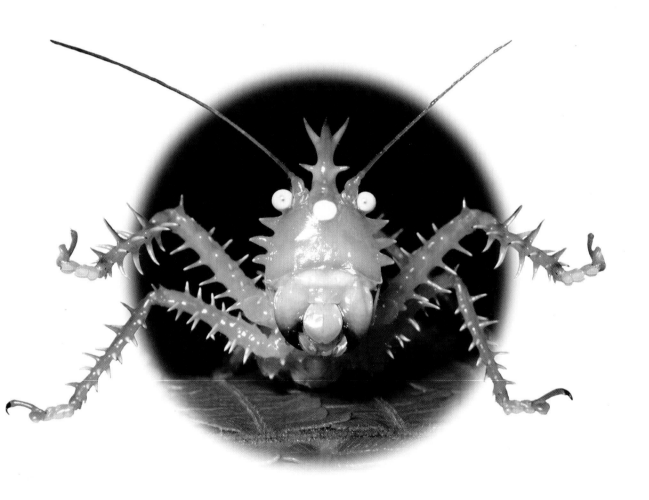

# KINGFISHER

a Houghton Mifflin Company imprint
222 Berkeley Street
Boston, Massachusetts 02116
www.houghtonmifflinbooks.com

First published in 2006
2 4 6 8 10 9 7 5 3
2TR/0206/PROSP/RNB/140MA/F

LIBRARY OF CONGRESS CATALOGING-IN-PUBLICATION DATA
has been applied for.

ISBN 0-7534-5933-7
ISBN 978-07534-5933-1

Printed in China

**Senior editor:** Belinda Weber
**Coordinating editor:** Caitlin Doyle
**Designer:** Joanne Brown
**Cover designer:** Poppy Jenkins
**Picture manager:** Cee Weston-Baker
**DTP coordinator:** Lisa Hancock
**DTP operator:** Claire Cessford
**Artwork archivist:** Wendy Allison
**Production controller:** Jessamy Oldfield
**Proofreader and indexer:** Sheila Clewley

Acknowledgments
The publishers would like to thank the following for permission to reproduce their material. Every care has been taken
to trace copyright holders. However, if there have been unintentional omissions or failure to trace copyright holders,
we apologize and will, if informed, endeavor to make corrections in any future edition.
b = bottom, c = center, l = left, t = top, r = right

Cover Corbis/Zefa; 1 Frank Lane Picture Agency (FLPA)/Michael & Patricia Fogden; 2–3 Nature Picture Library (Naturepl)/Ingo
Arndt; 4–5 Corbis/Michael & Patricia Fogden; 6–7 FLPA/Minden; 7tr FLPA/Panda Photo; 7br Getty Dorling Kindersley; 8l
FLPA/Foto Natura; 8–9 FLAP/Roger Wilmshurst; 9r FLPA/B. Borrell Casals; 10b Ardea/Pascal Goetgheluck; 10–11 FLPA/Minden;
11tr Ardea/Steve Hopkin; 12 FLPA/Minden; 12–13 Naturepl/Ingo Arndt; 13tr Natural History Picture Agency (NHPA)/ Stephen
Dalton; 14cr NHPA/James Carmichael; 14cl FLPA/Foto Natura; 14bl Naturepl/Duncan McEwan; 15 Photolibrary.com; 16
NHPA/Paal Hermansen; 17t Ardea/Steve Hopkin; 17b FLPA/Minden; 18 Photolibary.com; 19t Photolibrary.com; 19b FLPA/Derek
Middleton; 20bl Naturepl/Premaphotos; 21tr FLPA/Richard Becker; 21b FLPA/Foto Natura; 22lc Science Photo Library
(SPL)/Susumu Nishinaga; 22bl Naturepl/Warwick Sloss; 23t Ardea/Steve Hopkin; 23cl SPL/Nuridsany & Perennou; 23cr
SPL/Susumu Nishinaga; 23br Naturepl/Ross Hoddinott; 24–25 Naturepl/Premaphotos; 24b FLPA/Foto Natura; 25br Ardea/John
Mason; 26 Corbis/Anthony Bannister; 26bl FLPA/Foto Natura; 27b Naturepl/Martin Dohrn; 28cl Alamy; 28br Photolibrary.com;
29 Naturepl/Michael Durham; 29b Getty NGS; 30 Corbis/Anthony Bannister; 31t NHPA/George Bernard; 31b FLPA/Foto Natura;
32 FLPA/Minden 33tr FLPA/Derek Middleton; 33b FLPA/Minden; 34–35 Photolibrary.com; 34b Photolibrary.com; 35tr
Photolibrary.com; 36 Photolibrary.com; 37t Naturepl/Martin Dohrn; Corbis/Anthony Bannister; 38 Alamy/Peter Arnold Inc.; 39t
Alamy/Robert Pickett; 39b Alamy/Maximilian Weinzierl; Getty Imagebank

Commissioned photography on pages 42–47 by Andy Crawford
Projectmaker and photoshoot coordinator: Jo Connor
Thank you to models Alex Bandy, Alastair Carter, Tyler Gunning, and Lauren Signist

Kingfisher Young Knowledge

# Insects

## Barbara Taylor

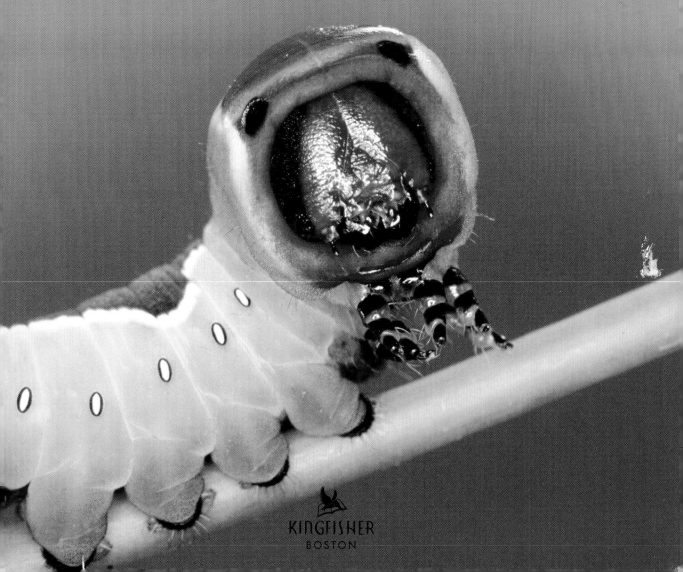

KINGFISHER
BOSTON

# Contents

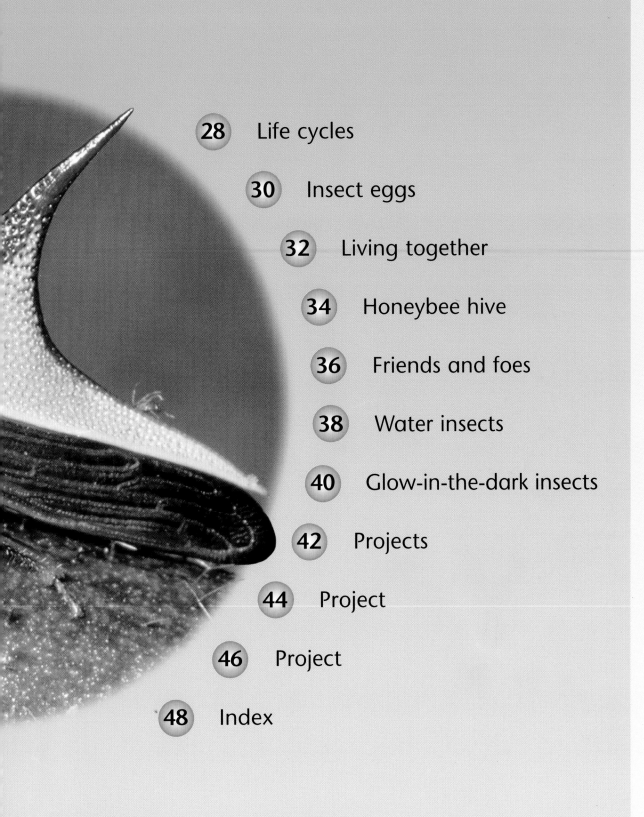

# What is an insect?

An insect is a small animal with six legs and three parts to its body. A hard outer skeleton covers and protects an insect's body like a suit of armor.

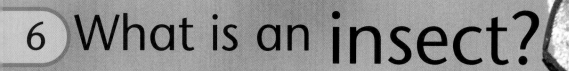

*Dragonfly*

## Wonderful wings

Most insects have one or two pairs of wings. Their wings are thin flaps that are made from their outer body covering. The wings are connected to the thorax, the middle part of an insect's body.

*skeleton—a structure that supports an animal's body*

The
on E
400 r
ago—
people
This inse
in the sti
oozed fro
was preser
millions of

## Not an insect!

Spiders, such as this
common house spider,
are not insects. Spiders have
eight legs and only
have two parts to
their bodies. Their head
and thorax are connected.
They do not have wings.

*Earth—the planet on which we live*

s of
**ts**

llions of
bes of insects,
divided into
ch as beetles,
s and moths, bees,
ies, and bugs.

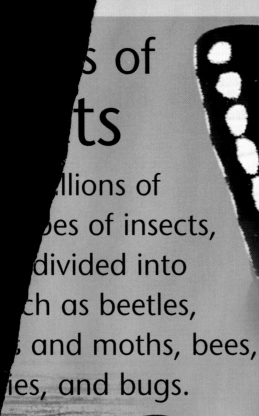

## Wasps

Wasps belong to a group
of insects that also includes
bees and ants. A wasp has
a narrow "waist," and it
folds its wings along the
sides of its body.

**bugs**—*insects with sucking mouthparts*

## Flies

A fly only has one pair of wings, but it can fly very well. The fly group includes mosquitoes and bluebottles, like this one.

## Butterflies

Butterflies and moths have wings that are covered in tiny scales, which overlap like tiles on a roof. Butterflies, such as this swallowtail, are usually brightly colored and fly around during the day.

**flies**—insects with only one pair of wings

# Big and small insects

Most insects are small beasts—even the biggest insects could sit in your hand. Their small size means that they can live in small spaces and do not need much food.

## Tiny fleas

Fleas live in the fur of mammals or the feathers of birds. They have claws for clinging on tight and long legs for jumping from one animal to another.

*mammals*—hairy animals that feed their babies on the mother's milk

## Nasty nits

Head lice thrive in the warmth of human hair, sucking the blood from our skin. Female head lice glue their eggs onto the hair. These eggs are known as nits.

## Giant weta

Wetas are giant crickets that live in New Zealand. They probably grew into such huge insects because there were no large predatory mammals to eat them.

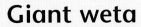

*predators—animals that hunt and eat other animals*

# Athletic insects

Some insects are like human athletes. They are incredible sprinters, high jumpers, or weight lifters. Insects use their athletic powers to find food or mates—or even just to stay alive.

### Weight lifting
One of these male rhinoceros beetles has managed to lift the other one completely off the ground! He wins the chance to mate with the females.

**mate**—*to breed or reproduce*

## High jump

Insects that are good at high-jumping, such as this leafhopper, usually have long back legs that are powered by strong muscles in the thorax.

## Sprinting

Long legs help insects take big strides and sprint (move fast). The legs of this tiger beetle are much longer than its body. Three of its six legs touch the ground almost all the time.

*muscles*—*parts of the body that produce movement*

# Wonder wings

Insects were the first animals that were able to fly. Flying helps insects find food or mates and escape danger, but it also uses up a lot of energy.

### Long journeys

Monarch butterflies fly thousands of miles each year to escape the cold winters in Canada. These long journeys are called migration.

### Wing covers

Beetles, such as this ladybug, have two pairs of wings. When a beetle lands, its hard front wings cover and protect its delicate flying wings.

*flexible—able to bend without breaking*

## Strong wings

A network of veins found inside of an insect's wings makes them strong and flexible. You can see the veins very clearly on this cicada's wings.

**veins**—*narrow tubes that are full of blood*

# Cunning colors

Dull colors help insects hide from predators. Bright colors or patterns warn predators to stay away because that insect is poisonous or harmful.

## Warning colors

The bright red spots on this burnet moth are a warning message, saying: "Don't eat me, I contain a deadly poison."

## Fake wasp

The wasp beetle cannot sting and is not dangerous. Predators leave it alone because they think that it is a real wasp and might sting them.

## Hide-and-seek

Many insects use camouflage in order to hide from predators by looking like the plants that they live on. This thorn bug even has a pretend camouflaged thorn on its back!

*camouflage—a shape, color, or pattern that helps an animal hide*

# Fighting back

From sharp jaws to painful stingers and chemical weapons, insects have many ways of fighting back when they are attacked by predators.

### Ready, aim, fire!

Bombardier beetles spray boiling-hot poisons at their enemies. The poisons are mixed together inside the beetles' bodies when danger threatens.

### Horrible hissing

If these cockroaches are disturbed, they make a loud, hissing noise by pushing air out from breathing holes in their sides. This startles predators, such as spiders, and gives the cockroaches time to escape.

*stinger—a sharp needle on an insect's body used for injecting poisons*

## Battling beetle

The rove beetle, or devil's coach horse beetle, defends itself by curling its abdomen over its back like a scorpion. At the same time the beetle gives off a terrible smell and snaps its jaws together.

*abdomen*—*the long part of an insect's body that contains its digestive system*

# Insect senses

An insect's senses of sight, touch, smell, and hearing are vital to its survival. These senses are often much better than our own, but they work in different ways.

## Touch and smell

Insects use their antennae to touch and smell their surroundings. This weevil's antennae have special hairs at the ends to detect smells.

*senses—the ways an animal detects its surroundings*

## Head fans

Scarab beetles fan out their antennae when they fly, in order to increase their size. This helps them detect any smells.

## Eye spy

The big eyes of this fly are made up of thousands of very small eyes. They can see in many different directions at the same time.

**antennae**—long, thin structures on an insect's head used for touching and smelling

# Hungry insects

Some insects, such as cockroaches, eat almost anything, but most insects feed on particular types of foods. Their mouthparts help them hold and chop up solid foods or suck up liquids.

### Spongy mouth

Flies turn their food into a soupy mush and then use a spongy pad (left) to mop up their meal. Flies can also taste their food with their feet!

*mouthparts—structures on the head that are used for feeding*

## Jagged jaws

Predatory insects need sharp, spiky jaws for holding and chopping up their prey. The jaws of insects that chew plants are less sharp so that they can grind and mash up their food.

## Drinking straws

Butterflies and moths feed on liquid food such as flower nectar or rotting fruit. They suck up their food through a tube, called a proboscis, that works like a straw.

*nectar—a sweet liquid that is made by plants*

# Nibbling plants

All the different parts
of plants are eaten
by insects. Some
plant-eating insects
are farmers, growing
their own crops and
harvesting the seeds.

## Leaves for lunch

Leaves do not contain
enough nutrients, so insects
need to eat a lot of them.
Grasshoppers are messy
eaters, often tearing the
leaves as they eat them.

*fungi—living things that cannot make their own food*

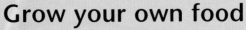

## Grow your own food

Leaf-cutter ants, or leaf-cutting ants, chew up pieces of leaves and use them to make a mushy compost pile. They grow fungi on the compost so that they always have plenty to eat.

## Wood for dinner

Wood contains even fewer nutrients than leaves, but some insects eat it. The larvae of deathwatch beetles spend many years eating damp wood before turning into adults, like this one.

*larvae—young insects that hatch out of eggs*

# Insect hunters

Insects hunt in three main ways: they may chase after their prey, jump out from a hiding place, or set a trap to catch a meal. Most insects hunt alone, but a few search in groups.

## Clever disguise

Many mantises look like leaves. They stay very still, then they shoot out their long front legs to grab a passing insect. A mantis has sharp jaws to slice up its prey and scoop out its soft insides.

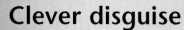

*prey*—*an animal that is killed or eaten by another animal*

## Soupy snacks

Robber flies catch flying insects with their long, hairy legs. Then they turn the insides of the prey into a soupy liquid and suck up their meal.

## All together now

Army ants from tropical America hunt in large groups. The ants help each other catch and kill their prey. These army ants have caught a centipede.

*tropical*—*an area close to the equator with very hot, dry weather*

# Life cycles

Many insects have four stages in their life cycles—egg, larva, pupa, and adult. Insect groups that develop in this way include beetle: butterflies, moths, flies, fleas, bees, and ants.

### 1 Egg

A female monarch butterfly lays her eggs underneath the leaves of milkweed plants. Within one week the eggs hatch into stripy caterpillars.

### 2 Larva

The hungry caterpillar eats and eats and eats. It sheds its skin several times as it grows. This is called molting.

*caterpillars—the wormlike larvae of butterflies and moths*

### 3 Pupa

When the caterpillar is big enough, it turns into a chrysalis, or pupa. Inside the pupa the body of the caterpillar changes into the body of a butterfly.

### 4 Adult

The crysalis splits open, and the adult butterfly pulls itself free. The butterfly pumps blood into its wings to stretch them out and waits for its wings to dry. Then it flies away to look for a mate.

**pupa**—*a protective case around a developing adult insect*

# Insect eggs

Almost all insects start their lives as eggs. The eggs are usually laid on or close to food and are hidden away from predators and bad weather. Very few insects take care of their eggs.

## Easy meals

Dung beetles shape animal dung into a ball, which they then roll to a safe place. The female lays her eggs inside the dung ball so that the young will have food when they hatch.

*hatch*—to come out of an egg

## Caring parent

Female earwigs guard their eggs for months until they hatch. When they do hatch, the babies look like their mother, but without wings.

## Male on guard

This male damselfly is holding the female's neck while she lays her eggs on the stems of underwater plants. When the eggs hatch, the young live underwater for the first year.

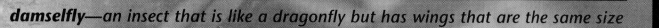

*damselfly—an insect that is like a dragonfly but has wings that are the same size*

# Living together

Most insects live alone, but a few types live and work together in groups. These are called social insects. All ants and termites—as well as some bees and wasps—are social insects.

**Royal ruler**
A big, fat queen termite lays all the eggs in a nest. The smaller worker termites carry her eggs away and bring food for their queen.

*social*—*living in a group with others of the same species, or type*

## Paper nest

Paper wasps make their nests by chewing up wood and mixing it with their spit in order to make wasp "paper." Inside the nest there are many tiny boxes, called cells, where young wasps can develop.

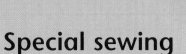

## Special sewing

Weaver ants work together as a team to make a nest out of leaves that are glued together with sticky silk. One ant working on its own would not be strong enough to do this.

**queen**—*a female that lays the eggs in a group of social insects*

# Honeybee hive

People build artificial nests, called hives, for honeybees. The honeybees make honey from the nectar of flowers and mix it with their spit. Beekeepers take this honey for people to eat.

## Wax city

Honeybees use wax that is made inside their bodies to build rows of six-sided boxes called cells. These cells fit together tightly to make a thin sheet called a honeycomb.

*artificial—man-made*

## Queen bee

The big bee in the middle of this picture is a queen honeybee. She lays all the eggs in a honeybee hive.

## Beekeeper

Beekeepers lift the honeycombs out to check on the honey and the baby bees that are inside. They wear special clothing to protect them from bee stings.

*beekeeper*—*a person who takes care of honeybee hives*

# Friends and foes

Many insects are our friends because they help flower seeds develop and are an important link in food chains. However, some insects cause problems because they eat crops or carry diseases.

## Pollen carriers

Many flowers rely on insects to carry a yellow dust, called pollen, to other flowers of the same type. Pollen has to mix with the eggs inside flowers before seeds can develop.

**foes**—enemies

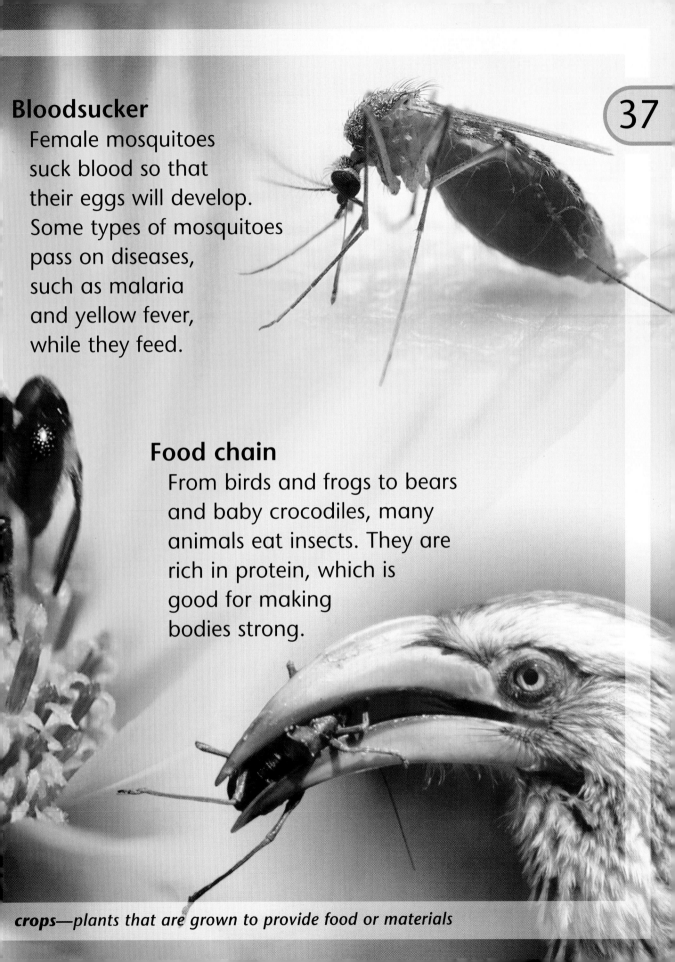

## Bloodsucker

Female mosquitoes
suck blood so that
their eggs will develop.
Some types of mosquitoes
pass on diseases,
such as malaria
and yellow fever,
while they feed.

## Food chain

From birds and frogs to bears
and baby crocodiles, many
animals eat insects. They are
rich in protein, which is
good for making
bodies strong.

*crops—plants that are grown to provide food or materials*

# Water insects

Many insects live in freshwater, where there is plenty of food and protection from predators. Some insects skim along the surface, some swim, and others lurk at the bottom.

## Spare air

Large diving beetles collect air from the surface of the water. They store the air under their wing covers so that they can breathe while they are underwater.

*freshwater—the water in lakes, streams, ponds, and puddles*

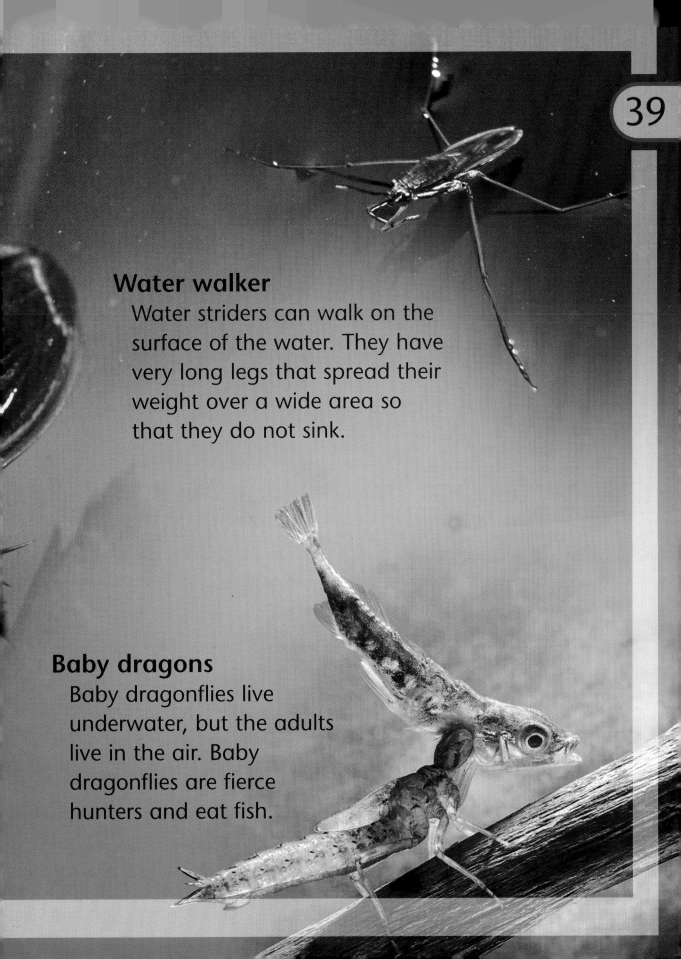

## Water walker

Water striders can walk on the
surface of the water. They have
very long legs that spread their
weight over a wide area so
that they do not sink.

## Baby dragons

Baby dragonflies live
underwater, but the adults
live in the air. Baby
dragonflies are fierce
hunters and eat fish.

# Glow-in-the-dark insects

Insects glow in the dark to attract prey or a mate, warn other insects about danger, or tell predators that they taste bad.

### Come and get me

Fireflies and glowworms are beetles that come out at night. Some of these beetles glow all the time, while others flash their "lights" on and off in a particular pattern. These light signals are used to attract a mate.

*glowworms—wingless female beetles that glow in the dark*

## Cave curtains

Small flies in New Zealand shine their lights down sticky strands that hang down from the roofs of caves. Prey insects are attracted to the glowing curtain and become trapped in the strands.

## Glowing bugs

A firefly produces a short burst of light when a gas, called oxygen, mixes with chemicals inside its abdomen. This works in a similar way to the glow-in-the-dark light sticks you see around Halloween.

*fireflies*—also called "lightning bugs"—glowing, nighttime beetles

# Bucket home

## Bug sleepover

Make a home for the bugs that live close to you. Draw pictures of the bugs that crawl inside and write their names down.

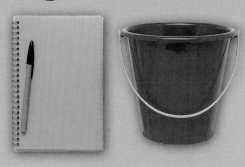

**1**

### You will need
- Plastic bucket
- Pen and notepad
- Stones, leaves, and grass

Find a damp, shady place close to your home. Turn the bucket upside down and balance it on a pile of stones, leaves, and grass. Leave it overnight and see if any creatures crawl inside of it.

*When you have finished, remember to let the animals go.*

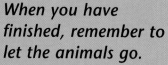

# Butterfly patterns

## Paint a butterfly

The patterns on one wing of a butterfly are the same as on the other side. Paint your own butterfly with matching sides.

### You will need

- Cardboard
- Pencil
- Scissors
- Paint
- Paintbrush
- Pipe cleaners

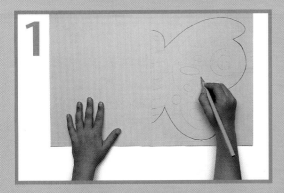

**1**

Fold the cardboard in half, then open it up flat. Use the pencil to draw the outline of half of a butterfly on one side of the fold.

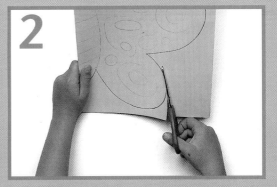

**2**

Fold the cardboard in half so that you can still see your pencil outline. Then carefully cut out the butterfly shape.

*Open the cardboard to see the whole butterfly and use pipe cleaners for its antennae.*

**3**

Open up the cardboard and paint one side with thick paint. Then fold your butterfly in half again and press down hard.

# Insect models

## Make a ladybug

Use papier-mâché to make a model of a giant ladybug. Paint the model red and black so that it looks just like a real ladybug. A ladybug's bright colors warn predators that it is poisonous and tastes bad.

### You will need
- Balloon
- Petroleum jelly
- Paintbrush
- Newspaper
- Wallpaper paste
- Scissors
- Paint
- Pipe cleaners
- Glue or tape

**1** Ask an adult to help you blow up a balloon. Spread a thick layer of petroleum jelly all over the balloon, then wash your hands.

**2** Cover the entire balloon with strips of newspaper. Brush wallpaper paste over the paper and repeat this about five times.

**3**

**4**

Put the balloon in a warm place to dry. When the surface is hard, use the scissors to carefully cut the balloon in half.

Paint the balloon with ladybug colors. Use pipe cleaners to make the legs and attach them with glue or tape.

*Look in books to see if there are any different colored ladybugs and paint the other papier-mâché shape in those colors.*

# Bug mobile

## Make a mobile

Hang this colorful mobile close to a window—or even outside—and watch the bugs fly around the flower as the breeze blows.

*Ladybug*

### You will need

- Colored cardboard
- Pencil
- Scissors
- Paintbrush
- Paint
- Thin wire
- String
- Tracing paper
- Strong thread
- Apron

**1** Draw a large flower shape onto colored cardboard and cut around the edge. Paint the flower with colors that you like.

**2** Ask an adult to help you make a circle out of wire. Tie four long pieces of string to the wire and knot the ends so that the mobile can hang.

**3**

Trace or copy the bugs on these pages or draw your own onto the cardboard. Cut them out and paint them to look like bugs.

**4**

Ask an adult to make small holes in your flower and bugs so that you can tie them to the wire circle. Your mobile is now ready to hang.

Bee

Shield bug

Dragonfly

# Index